PROFILE OF THE
DUCHESSES

Dirty, dishevelled but still going strong — a 'Duchess' in wartime.
British Rail (LMR)

Queen Elizabeth at Beattock, August 1953.
Eric Treacy

PROFILE OF THE DUCHESSES

Compiled by

David Jenkinson

'Returned to service, 1980' is the new entry on No. 46229's history card!
David Eatwell

Oxford Publishing Co.

©OPC and D. Jenkinson 1982

SBN 86093 176 5

Cover Photograph: *Duchess of Hamilton* heads for York with the Hadrian Pullman at Mossley on 18th July 1981.

Jim Carter

Published by
Oxford Publishing Co.,
Link House,
West Street,
Poole, Dorset.

PREFACE

To say that I was pleased with the reaction to *Power of the Duchesses* is to put it mildly. I have always had a high regard, coupled with not a little sentiment, for these splendid machines but I was highly delighted to find that my enthusiasm was shared by so many who were willing to purchase the book. Consequently, both I and the publisher felt that an encore in the 'Profile' series might well prove more acceptable than a reprint of the first book, provided it was not simply the same mixture as before. This time, therefore, I have chosen to feature each member of the class in turn rather than choose another collection of 'best Duchess' pictures. The aim has been to give a potted biography of each locomotive together with a representative collection of views showing each engine in several of its different guises. If, by seeking to meet this objective, I have at times sacrificed photographic impact in the interest of variety, I hope that my motives will be understood.

I gave a full summary of the class and its principal changes in *Power of the Duchesses*, so I will not repeat those details here. However, I have included short introductory sections on tenders, boilers and depot allocations as a sort of 'hors d'oeuvre' to tickle the palate, as it were, for this second picture book devoted to Stanier's design masterpiece. As usual I am deeply indebted to all those photographers whose work I have attempted to synthesise in an interesting way. If I have made any mistakes in crediting the pictures, may I apologise now and ask that I be informed via the publisher.

David Jenkinson
Knaresborough
1982

TENDER DESIGNS AND CHANGES

The 38 members of the 'Coronation' Class, to give the 'Duchesses' their correct terminology, were all coupled to high capacity 10 ton, 4,000 gallon standard Stanier tenders fitted with steam coalpushers. The tenders appeared small in relation to the locomotives but the LMS had abundant water troughs and the six-wheel design of tender enabled existing 70ft. turntables to be retained. Three main styles of tender were associated with the locomotives, as follows:

Type 'A' — Streamlined style, welded tank construction. (Locomotive Nos. 6220–9 and 35–52).
Type 'B' — Non-streamlined style, welded tank construction. (Locomotive Nos. 6230–4).
Type 'C' — Non-streamlined style, partially rivetted tank construction. (Locomotive Nos. 6253–6 and 46257).

Type 'C' came in two slight variants, depending on whether the cut-away at the front edge of the side tank was high up (Nos. 6253–5) or began immediately above the vertical handrail (Nos. 6256 and 46257). After de-streamlining, the ex-streamline tenders could always be recognised because they lacked both steps behind the rear wheels and vertical handrails at the rear of the side panels. On these tenders the side sheets were always higher at the front edge below the curved cut-away. They extended a few inches beyond the tender back where there was also a vertical ladder.

The LMS numbered its tenders separately from its locomotives and the distinctive numbers for the 'Duchess' tenders were as follows (in order of first allocation):

Type 'A'
Nos. 9703–7 fitted to locomotive Nos. 6220–4
Nos. 9743–7 fitted to locomotive Nos. 6225–9
Nos. 9798–815 fitted to locomotive Nos. 6235–52
Total = 28*

Type 'B'
Nos. 9748–52 fitted to locomotive Nos. 6230–4
Total = 5

Type 'C1' (high front edge)
Nos. 9816–7 and 10622 fitted to locomotive Nos. 6253–5
Type 'C2' (low front edge)
Nos. 10623–4 fitted to locomotive Nos. 6256 and 46257
Total (Types C1 and C2) = 5

*The last four were fitted to non-streamlined engines Nos. 6249–52

Plate 1: (left to right) 'Duchess' tenders type A (No. 46230), type B (No. 46236), type C1 (No. 46255) and type C2 (No. 46257). See text for amplification of details.

Over the years 16 locomotives always retained their original tenders while another 9 had only one change. The other 13 members of the class underwent many tender changes. The most 'travelled' tender was No. 9749 (originally fitted to No. 6231) which operated with no fewer than six locomotives, finishing its time behind No. 46246. Likewise, the most variable locomotive was No. 6242 which had no fewer than eight tender changes involving six different tenders after the first allocation!

In most cases tender changes were like for like (often straight exchanges following attention in works) but in a few cases non-streamlined tenders ran behind streamlined or de-streamlined engines (and vice versa). Apart from the four wartime non-streamlined engines (Nos. 6249–52) which ran throughout with streamlined tenders, which had already been constructed, there were only three semi-permanent 'mis-matches'. Engine Nos. 6230/1 ran from 1945 until scrapping with ex-streamlined tenders while No. 6223 ran from 1946 until withdrawal with the non-streamlined tender originally fitted to No. 6230. The original tender of No. 6231 migrated round a little but spent its longest single allocation behind No. 46247 in the 1950s. Fuller details are given with each locomotive considered.

BOILERS

There were 44 boilers in existence for the 38 'Duchesses' and all were totally interchangeable. Boiler changes usually took place during heavy general repairs and while most of the class entered service with brand new boilers, three (Nos. 6245/7–8) started their working lives with recently overhauled boilers originally built for earlier members of the class. A brief summary is given here. More detailed information is given later with each locomotive.

Boiler Nos.	Details
9937–41	Built new with locomotive Nos. 6220–4
10287–306	Built new with locomotive Nos. 6225–44 but not fitted in corresponding numerical order.
10637–46	Built during the early 1940s, mostly for stock, but last three fitted new to locomotive Nos. 6249, 6246, 6250, respectively
10693–4	Built new with locomotive Nos. 6251–2
12470–4	Built new with locomotive Nos. 6253–6 and 46257
13043–4	Built for stock in 1949-50

DEPOT ALLOCATIONS

Throughout their lives, the 'Duchesses' were almost exclusively allocated to one of four depots: Camden (1B), Crewe North (5A), Carlisle (Upperby) (12B) and Glasgow (Polmadie) (27A) (66A after nationalisation). Apart from these four, Edge Hill (8A) and Holyhead (7C) had small allocations for short periods from time to time, generally involving one or two engines for a month or so. Occasionally the Carlisle engines worked from Kingmoor (12A) and for a time during the BR period Upperby carried the 12A code which can cause confusion when trying to distinguish between these two Carlisle sheds.

The pattern of allocations was straightforward. All new locomotives up to and including No. 6248 went first to Camden (apart from a few which spent a month or so working up at Crewe first). As the class grew in numbers some of the earlier members were transferred to Crewe and Polmadie. Carlisle was the last depot to receive a major allocation and this was not until late 1946 and 1947 when the last series (Nos. 6253–46257) went to Camden from new thus allowing some further re-allocation of earlier locomotives. All locomotives were based at Camden at some time in their career although Nos. 6251/2 spent very little of their time there. Only four engines (Nos. 6249–52) did not start their regular working lives at Camden. The appended table gives the general pattern (excluding short-term moves) and the following notes amplify the picture at the four main depots until scrapping started in 1963. During the last year or two there were several re-allocations to depots not shown on the engine history cards.

SUMMARY OF 'DUCHESS' 4-6-2 ALLOCATION AT DEPOTS AS AT AUTUMN OF THE YEARS SHOWN BELOW

Depot	37	38	39 (a)	40	41	42	43	44	45	46	47	48	49	50	51	52	53	54	55	56	57	58	59	60	61	62	63	64 (b)	64 (b)
Camden and/or Willesden	5	14	19	12	12	12	20	16	16	15	14	14	12†	12†	14	15	15	15	15	15	14	9	8	7	6	7	3	3	(3)
Crewe North		1*	1*	5*	5*	5	1	5	5	6	8	7	10	10	8	10	9	9	9	10	12	15	11	11	10	9	7	7	(7)
Polmadie				8	8	8	8	12	12	9	9	9	9	9	9	9	9	9	9	9	9	7	7	7	9	9	–	–	
Upperby										6	6	6	7	7	7	4	5	4	4	4	3	7	12	12	12	12	10	10	(9)
Edge Hill												2						1	1					1	1	1	1	1	
Holyhead																											1	1	(1)
TOTAL:	5	15	20	25	25	25	29	33	33	36	37	38	38	38	38	38	38	38	38	38	38	38	38	38	38	38	22	22	(20)

Notes:
(a) During 1939-40 as new locomotives came into service, there were almost simultaneous transfers from Camden to Polmadie and Crewe but for a brief period (end of 1939) all except No. 6229 were at Camden.
(b) 1964 distribution shows start of year *and* final position (in brackets) at time of September 1964 demise of whole class.
* Including No. 6229 (in USA).
† Temporary slight reduction, possibly because of introduction of LMS Diesels 10,000/10,001?

Camden (1B) was always the major 'Duchess' depot until the late 1950s. Until the outbreak of war, all members (except No. 6229, temporarily in the USA until 1942) were based there and it was common practice after the war until well into the 1950s for the other English depots to release some engines to Camden during the summer months. Surprisingly, only four members of the class (Nos. 6239–40, 6245 and 6247) were permanently associated with Camden, although several others (e.g. Nos. 6237, 6241, 6244, 6256 and 46257) spent what might be considered their 'prime' as 1B engines until the advent of main-line diesels. When Camden closed in 1961, the remaining London 'Duchesses' moved to Willesden.

Crewe North (5A) Apart from having some of the new engines allocated for a month or so during 1938–9, Crewe did not receive its first regular 'Duchess' allocation until mid-1940 when the first five red streamliners were based there (four ex-Camden and No. 6229 on its return from the USA.

These were replaced later in the war but it was not until the late 1940s that as many as eight to ten engines were continuously allocated. Of those which went to Crewe, only one (No. 6235) spent the whole of its remaining life there (from 1944), although No. 6248 was a virtually permanent resident from mid-1948 onwards.

Polmadie (27A, later 66A) Glasgow (Polmadie) was the second depot after Camden to receive a permanent allocation and the men must have liked the engines they received, since most of those transferred were never again re-allocated before scrapping! In early 1940, the five blue streamliners (Nos. 6220–4) and three of the red non-streamliners (Nos. 6230–2) went to Glasgow and, apart from Nos. 6220–1 in the final years, remained there until the end. The other permanent member of the 'Polmadie

Club' was No. 46227, which was transferred in 1948, and also remained until scrapping. During 1945–6, the allocation was temporarily increased to twelve, including three new engines (Nos. 6249–51) and No. 6242. Nos. 6242/9 returned again in the early 1960s but no other members of the class were ever based in Scotland.

Carlisle Upperby (12B, later 12A, then 12B again) From late 1946, Carlisle always had a regular handful of 'Duchesses' on allocation and, of course, during the final years, Carlisle became the major depot for the class. No single member of the class remained at Carlisle throughout the 1946–64 period but Nos. 6226, 6238 and 6255 were only rarely absent, while No. 6228 was a semi-permanent member, except for a period at Crewe from 1957–9.

Of the locomotives not traditionally associated with one particular depot, the most frequent transferee was No. 6251 which, between lengthy spells at Upperby and Crewe, was involved in seven transfers between 1948 and 1950 and no fewer than fourteen between 1954 and 1957. Further allocation details are given with each locomotive individually.

Footnote:
Mileages I have quoted for each engine its average annual revenue mileage for the years during which records were maintained. This was not always for the whole life of the locomotive but averaging does seem to give a better measure of performance than absolute mileage figures. It is noticeable that engines based at Polmadie ran fewer miles than the others and this is likely to be a function of their frequent rostering over shorter distance journeys than the English-based engines rather than reflecting any basic differences in quality. The overall class average was just over 65,000 revenue miles per locomotive per year.

No. 6220 CORONATION

Doyen of the class and first of the blue streamliners, *Coronation* first drew attention to the potential of the design with a hair-raising 114 mph descent of Madeley bank in 1937 on the press run of the 'Coronation Scot'. Two years later she exchanged identity with No. 6229 and ran for several years as *Duchess of Hamilton*, identities reverting in 1943.

Thereafter, No. 6220 led a fairly straightforward life. Initially based at Camden, she spent most of her time at Polmadie and moved to Crewe in 1958 where she remained, save for a short spell at Upperby in 1960.

Summary:

Built: Crewe, 1st June, 1937; total cost £11,641
Tenders: 9703 (new); 9803 (1944); 9703 (1944); 9804 (1946); 9705 (1949)
Boilers: first — 9937; last —10296 (1960); number of boiler changes: 7
Main Shed Allocations: Camden (1937); Polmadie (12/39); Crewe (9/58)
Average Annual Mileage: 58,741
Withdrawn: week ending 20th April, 1963

Plates 2 & 3: Coronation in her earlier years. To the right, the engine heads the southbound 'Coronation Scot' down Shap bank in 1937 with the regulator obviously open. Below, in 1948, she is seen de-streamlined on the southbound climb to Shap wearing 1946 LMS livery but carrying BR number.

British Rail (LMR) & Eric Treacy

Plates 4 to 6: (left) Polmadie often used its 4-6-2s for local Edinburgh–Glasgow trips and in the upper two views *Coronation* is seen on these workings at Slateford Junction and Edinburgh (Princes Street) respectively, in both cases wearing BR green livery. Note the change to full cylindrical smokebox which took place in December, 1955. Finally, during its last years, No. 46220, now Crewe-based, climbs Camden bank with a northbound train. The engine is still green but now carries the later BR emblem.

David Anderson (2) & R. C. Riley

Plate 7: (opposite) *Queen Elizabeth* seen ▷ climbing Camden bank with the down 'Coronation Scot' c1937–8.

Photomatic

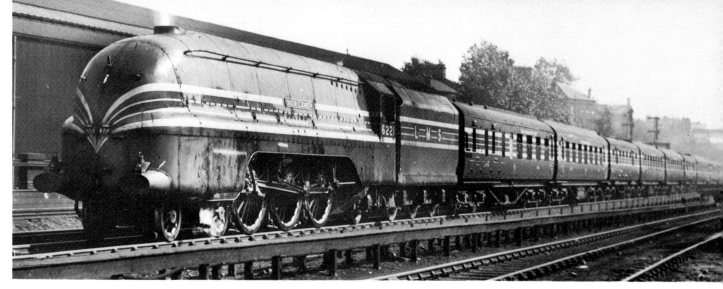

No. 6221 QUEEN ELIZABETH

The second blue streamliner had a somewhat similar history to *Coronation*. The only real difference was that, after leaving Polmadie in 1958, it shared its time between Crewe, Camden and Upperby.

Interestingly, *Queen Elizabeth* was unique in two odd respects. It was the only blue streamliner to be repainted red (in 1941) and it was also the only 'Duchess' to be fitted with a 'Princess Royal'-type tender (10 tons capacity but without coal pusher). This event occurred during its penultimate year in traffic.

Summary:
  Built: Crewe, 14th June, 1937; total cost £11,641
  Tenders. 9704 (new); 9816 (1961); 9359 ('Princess Royal' type, 1962)
  Boilers: first — 9938; last — 10298 (1961); number of boiler changes: 7
  Main Shed Allocations: Camden (1937); Polmadie (12/39); Crewe (7/58); Camden (6/59); Crewe (10/60); Upperby (4/62)
  Average Annual Mileage: 58,162
  Withdrawn: week ending 18th May, 1963

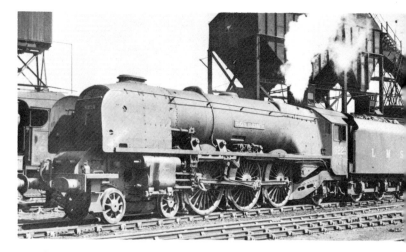

Plates 8 & 9: When de-streamlined early in 1946, No. 6221 ran in drab wartime black for a few months (seen at Crewe above). The view at Carlisle (below) taken in 1946, shows the style which was worn until early BR days.

Author's Collection & Gavin Wilson

Plate 10: This unusual high-level view of No. 46221 passing Kingmoor in the 1950s gives a fine impression of the boilers of the 'Duchesses' and should be of help to modellers. *Queen Elizabeth* was one of the first to receive the full cylindrical smokebox — in 1952.

Eric Treacy

Plate 11: No. 46221 went to Upperby in early 1962 and is seen here on empty stock duty at Chester during the short period it was coupled to tender No. 9816 before receiving the 'Princess' type later in 1962. The livery is BR green with later tender emblem.

Jim Carter

No. 6222 QUEEN MARY

None of the 'Duchesses' led easy lives but some seemed less in the headlines than others. *Queen Mary* was one such. Having spent its first two years at Camden, it went off to Polmadie in late 1939 and stayed there. Neither was it one of the more chameleon-like examples. It only wore four main liveries: LMS blue, LMS black, BR blue and BR green which, for a 'Duchess', was really quite restrained! It also held the somewhat dubious distinction of having the lowest average annual mileage of any member of the class. Its regulator handle is preserved — fitted to *Duchess of Hamilton*.

Summary:

    Built: Crewe, 22nd June, 1937; total cost £11,641
    Tenders: 9705 (new); 9804 (1949)
    Boilers: first — 9939; last 10289 (1959); number of
        boiler changes: 8
    Main Shed Allocations: Camden (1937); Polmadie (12/39)
    Average Annual Mileage: 55,723
    Withdrawn: week ending 26th October, 1963

Plate 12: All five blue streamliners worked the 'Coronation Scot' turn and turn about, unlike some of the Gresley LNER 'A4s' which, like *Silver Link*, tended to be semi-permanent fixtures on a particular train. *Queen Mary* is seen on duty at Willesden.

Locomotive Publishing Company

Plate 13: After the war, the de-streamlined engines all received the 1946 LMS livery in due course. Some, however, were experimented with and this view shows No. 6222, without boiler lining and with close-spaced 'LMS' set low on the tender, passing Headstone Lane with an up Glasgow—Euston sleeping car train.

British Rail (LMR)

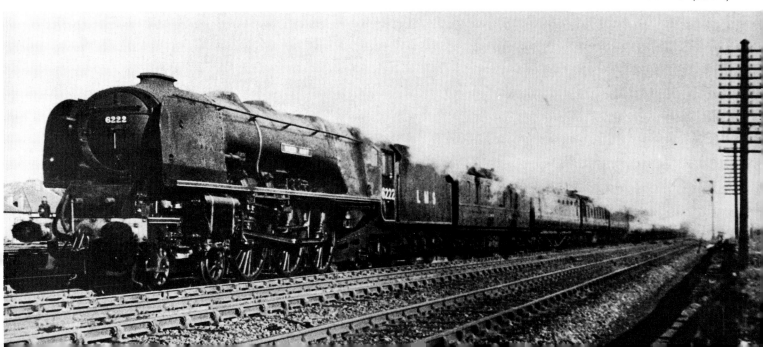

Plate 14: The Polmadie 'Duchesses' were often night birds since they had to cope with the heavy sleeping car and postal traffic from Glasgow to London for many years. *Queen Mary* is seen at Elvanfoot in the dusk with the up 'West Coast Postal'.

David Anderson

Plate 15: By 1961, diesels had taken over many 'Duchess' jobs but, in August 1961, *Queen Mary* was photographed with an up Perth–London train at Carlisle during a short period of temporary reversion to steam haulage.

S. C. Crook

No. 6223 PRINCESS ALICE

In terms of depot allocation and liveries carried, *Princess Alice* enjoyed an almost identical career to that of *Queen Mary*. However, in one respect, the locomotive was unique. In 1946, it received tender No. 9748 (originally built for *Duchess of Buccleuch*) and retained it for the rest of its working life. Other ex-streamliners were occasionally paired with non-streamline tenders but No. 6223 was the only one which, in effect, contracted a permanent marriage with an incompatible partner!

Summary:
Built: Crewe, 28th June, 1937; total cost £11,641
Tenders: 9706 (new); 9748 (1946)
Boilers: first — 9940; last — 10299 (1960); number of boiler changes: 9
Main Shed Allocations: Camden (1937); Polmadie (12/39)
Average Annual Mileage: 56,222
Withdrawn: October, 1963

Plate 16: During the 'Coronation Scot' years the blue streamliners were all based at Camden. *Princess Alice* is seen here at Hartford with the down train in 1939. Later the same year, she moved to Polmadie for good.

British Rail (LMR)

Plate 17: This quiet study of *Princess Alice* at Glasgow clearly shows the non-streamlined tender originally belonging to No. 6230. The date is not certain but the livery is believed to be BR blue which indicates some time between 1950 and 1952.

Photomatic

No. 6224 PRINCESS ALEXANDRA

The last of the blue streamliners, No. 6224, shared a similar career to that of Nos. 6222/3. After 2 years or so at Camden, the engine went to Polmadie in late 1939 and stayed there. It had a short flirtation with a non-streamlined tender (ex-6230) but then acquired tender 9706 (ex-6223) when *Princess Alice* also acquired a non-streamlined version. No. 6224 had the unrivalled distinction of having more boiler changes than any other member of the class — eleven in all!

Summary:
Built: Crewe, 13th July, 1938; total cost £11,641
Tenders: 9707 (new); 9748 (1945); 9706 (1946)
Boilers: first — 9941: last — 10288 (1962); number of boiler changes: 11
Main Shed Allocations: Camden (1937); Polmadie (12/39)
Average Annual Mileage: 56,091
Withdrawn: week ending 19th October, 1963

Plates 21 & 22: above, *Princess Alexandra* is seen in BR experimental blue livery c 1948 approaching Carlisle on the down 'Royal Scot' (also in experimental colours). Below, the same train is seen in standard red/cream livery behind a green No. 46224 at Kensal Green on 24th July, 1953.

Real Photographs & British Rail (LMR)

No. 6225 DUCHESS OF GLOUCESTER

It was 1938 when the 'Duchess' names began to appear and No. 6225 was the first. Regrettably, I never saw a streamliner in either blue or red but always imagine that the red ones must have looked better; and No. 6225 was the first of 14 thus painted. After the war *Duchess of Gloucester* was the engine selected for testing at Rugby and helped establish (with No. 6234) the 'most powerful' claim for the class. She was one of the most travelled members of the class (in terms of shed allocation) and spent considerable periods at the three main English depots including a spell at Holyhead in late 1939. This engine also has the distinction of accumulating the highest recorded total mileage of any member of the class — 1,742,624 — although several other engines may well have actually achieved higher totals. Unfortunately, records do not exist beyond 1958/9 for some of them.

Plate 23: The down 'Royal Scot' with 17 on — No. 6225 in charge — at Bushey in 1939. The red streamliners were given much more diverse and frequently more arduous jobs than the blue ones which tended to be kept for the 'Coronation Scot' during 1937–9. *Photomatic*

Summary:
Built: Crewe, 11th May, 1938; total cost £11,302
Tenders: 9743 (new); 9749 (1945); 9799 (1949)
Boilers: first — 10297; last — 10693 (1961); number of boiler changes: 9
Main Shed Allocations: Camden (1938); Holyhead (1939) Crewe (1940); Camden (1943); Crewe (1946); Camden (1947); Crewe (1949); Rugby (1955); Camden (1955); Upperby (1959)
Average Annual Mileage: 66,183
Withdrawn: week ending 12th September, 1964

Plate 24: No. 46225, de-streamlined in the early 1950s, near Berkhamsted with the 14 coach 'Mid-Day Scot' — another tough task in those days. She was a Crewe North engine at the time and painted BR green.
British Rail (LMR)

Plate 25: *Duchess of Gloucester* acquired a normal shaped smokebox in 1955 and, three years later, was one of 16 'Duchesses' painted BR red. During most of this period the engine was at Upperby. In this view it is seen near Wreay on Easter Monday, 1963, with a Birmingham train. Note the ex-LMS articulated coaches – vehicles two and three.

S. C. Crook

Plate 26: No. 46225 was one of the last survivors and in 1964 acquired the yellow cab-side stripe prohibiting service under the wire south of Crewe. By this time, freight was a common task for the surviving 'Duchesses' and this view shows the engine approaching Wreay with the 07.36 Carlisle to Cardiff goods in August, 1964, a month or so before scrapping.

S. C. Crook

Plate 27: Immaculately clean and probably quite new, No. 6226 ascends Camden bank past an unidentified 'Princess Royal' Class 4-6-2 c 1938/9.

Real Photographs

Plate 28: Duchess of Norfolk was one of several members of the class to receive experimental colours in 1948. In this view, taken less than a year after de-streamlining, No. 46226 is seen in LNWR black.

Real Photographs

No. 6226 DUCHESS OF NORFOLK

Duchess of Norfolk, like her three sisters Nos. 6225/7–8, spent her first eight years or so at Camden and Crewe. All four engines tended to be transferred as a group between these depots. At the end of 1946, however, No. 6226 was one of the first to go to Upperby on a regular basis and, apart, perhaps, from No. 6238, was the most permanent resident at Carlisle of all the 'Duchesses' shedded there.

Plate 29: In its final years No. 46226 was one of the sixteen engines wearing BR red livery as seen here in the early 1960s near Crawford on a lightweight London to Perth train. Note the 1920s vintage corridor composite at the head of the train.

David Anderson

This engine was also, for whatever it may signify, the first of sixteen 'Duchesses' never to be involved in any tender changing activities.

Summary:

Built: Crewe, 23rd May, 1938; total cost £11,302

Tender: 9744 throughout

Boilers: first — 10298; last — 10640 (1960); number of boiler changes: 9

Main Shed Allocations: Camden (1938); Holyhead (1939); Crewe (1940); Camden (1943); Upperby (1946); with short periods of detachment to Camden, Edge Hill and Crewe during 1951–7

Average Annual Mileage: 67,764

Withdrawn: week ending 12th September, 1964

Plate 30: The standard running-in turn for a new 'Duchess' was from Crewe to Shrewsbury and No. 6227 is seen here on such a journey in 1938. The picture clearly shows the method of taking water through a removable side panel in the streamline casing of the tender.

Real Photographs

No. 6227 DUCHESS OF DEVONSHIRE

Duchess of Devonshire had a similar career to that of No. 6226 for the first eight years of its life. In 1946, however, the pattern was broken and, by 1948, *Duchess of Devonshire* had taken up residence at Polmadie where it remained for the rest of its life. It shares the melancholy distinction of being one of the first three to be withdrawn (at the end of 1962), along with Nos. 46231/2.

Summary:

Built: Crewe, 7th June, 1938; total cost £11,302
Tender: 9745 throughout
Boilers: first — 10299; last — 9938 (1961); number of boiler changes: 8
Main Shed Allocations: Camden (1938); Holyhead (1939); Crewe (1940); Camden (1943); Upperby (1946); Crewe (1947); Polmadie (1948)
Average Annual Mileage: 57,658
Withdrawn: week ending 29th December, 1962

Plate 31: No. 46227 in experimental BR livery at Tebay in 1948/9. The engine was painted dark blue with LNWR lining but is later reported to have been repainted LNWR black. In this picture the colour scheme is not certain.

Photomatic

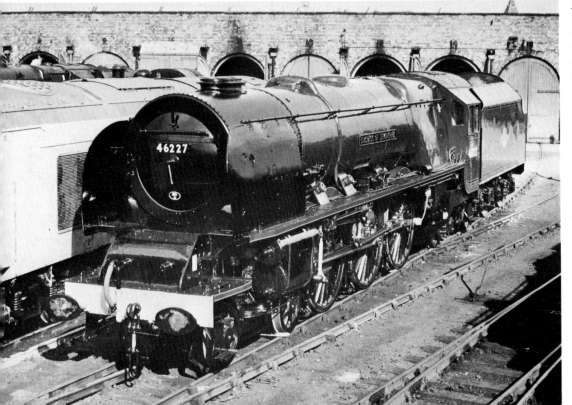

Plate 32: This view of No. 46227 shows the engine climbing Beattock with the down 'Royal Scot' during the period between 1951 and 1953 when it wore the BR standard blue livery.

Eric Treacy

Plate 33: Duchess of Devonshire was repainted green in 1953, simultaneously receiving a full cylindrical smokebox. This view shows it exworks in 1961 after its last heavy repair with the second BR tender emblem and overhead electrification warning labels.

Jim Carter

No. 6228 DUCHESS OF RUTLAND

No. 6228 was the last of the first quartet of red stream-liners. It generally moved along with the rest during its first eight years, after which it became a semi-permanent fixture at Upperby from 1946 until scrapped, except for a period at Crewe from 1957–9. Like many Carlisle 'Duchesses' it spent short summer seasons at Camden and Edge Hill on occasions and like most Upperby 4-6-2s, lasted until the end.

Summary:
Built: Crewe, 17th June 1938; total cost £11,302
Tender: 9746 throughout
Boilers: first – 10300; last – 10291 (1959); number of boiler changes: 8
Main Shed Allocations: Camden (1938); Longsight & Rugby (9/39); Holyhead (10/39); Crewe (1940); Camden (1943); Upperby (1946); Crewe (1957); Upperby (1959)
Average Annual Mileage: 68,002
Withdrawn: week ending 12th September, 1964

Plate 34: With tender partially de-streamlined and painted drab black overall, No. 6228 passes Golborne with a down express c1945-6. In this garb, the streamliners really were most uninspiring.

Coopers Railway Photographs

Plate 35: No. 6228 was an Upperby engine when de-streamlined. This view shows it late in 1947 in the full LMS post-war livery.

Real Photographs

Plate 36: No. 46228 carrying Crewe North shedplate and painted in BR maroon livery – the style in which it was withdrawn.

Author's Collection

Plate 37: *Duchess of Hamilton* at Bourne End, 1939, on the trial trip for the 1939 'Coronation Scot' USA tour, for which the engine was numbered 6220 and carried *Coronation* nameplates.

British Rail (LMR)

No. 6229 DUCHESS OF HAMILTON

In 1948 I was at Hest Bank, Lancashire, and got my first clearly remembered sight of a 'Duchess', storming south with the up 'Royal Scot'. The engine was *Duchess of Hamilton* and never in my wildest dreams did I think that some 30 years later I would be so closely involved with the re-birth of this same locomotive as the only preserved Stanier 'Duchess' in working order cleared for main line running on BR. It has been a great thrill to be involved with the project and I make no apology for devoting more than a fair share of pages to this engine, which bids fair to become the most photographed 'Duchess' of them all!

Summary:
  Built: Crewe, 7th September, 1938; total cost £11,302
    Tenders: 9747 (new); 9802 (1945)
  Boilers: first — 10306; last —10297 (1959); number of boiler changes: 8
  Main Shed Allocations: Crewe (1938); USA (1939–42); Crewe (1942); Camden (1943); Crewe (1947); Camden (1948); Crewe (1949); Camden (1952); Crewe (1960)
  Average Annual Mileage: (excluding USA): 67,241
  Returned to service: 10th May, 1980; based at National Railway Museum, York
  Withdrawn originally (for preservation by Butlins Ltd.) on 15th February 1964

Plates 38 to 40: These views show (left) No. 6229 under construction with No. 6228 nearly complete behind it at Crewe in 1939; left, below, undergoing trials in works grey, still properly named. The last picture (below) taken in early 1948, shows the newly de-streamlined engine in post-war LMS livery. *Duchess of Hamilton* was the next to the last of the class to be de-streamlined and, interestingly, the tender carries 'LMS', although the engine did not return to traffic until after 1947. This is how I first saw it and had it not been for the lack of sloping smokebox (as preserved) it would have been tempting to paint the engine in this style.

Photomatic & Real Photographs (2)

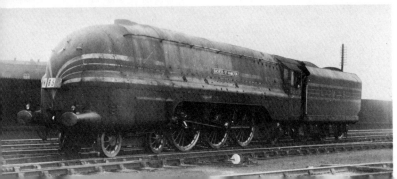

Plate 41: In early BR standard livery (probably blue, but maybe green) No. 46229 leaves Carlisle with a southbound train in the early 1950s.

Eric Treacy

Plate 42: This view at Crewe was taken between 1957 and 1958 when the engine had a fully cylindrical smokebox but was still in BR green.

Derek Cross

Plates 45 to 47: In *Power of the Duchesses* I speculated that we might once again hear the dark four-beat exhaust of a Stanier 'Duchess' in the northern hills. Well, it happened on the Settle to Carlisle line in November 1980. Northbound on 1st November the engine met trouble with greasy rails, but on 8th November coming south there was no problem. Above, the locomotive is prepared overnight at Upperby (how appropriate) and, right, re-starts from Garsdale with the 'Cumbrian Mountain Express'. Below on 21st March, 1981, the engine approaches Lunds viaduct in vile Settle to Carlisle weather on the northbound 'Cumbrian Mountain Express'.

David Eatwell (2) and Jim Carter

Plates 48 & 49: Once restored, No. 46229 was in great demand and, a few days after the first Settle to Carlisle trip, was helping celebrate the 150th anniversary of 'Mail by Rail' on 11th November, 1980. Left, the willing volunteer support crewe bring coal forward at Manchester Victoria prior to the run via Huddersfield to Leeds and York. Below, the engine was making a stupendous noise as the train climbed to Diggle through Greenfield. I was in the leading coach — magic!

David Eatwell & Larry Goddard

Plate 50: No. 46229 nears the summit at Standedge tunnel on 11th November, 1980. The leading vehicle is National Railway Museum's preserved LMS (ex-LNWR) Royal Train brake and the next vehicle is the Post Office exhibition mail coach.

David Eatwell

Plate 51: In 1981, No. 46229 had two more trips on the Settle to Carlisle line. Possibly the best of the runs was southbound on 28th March (right) when Appleby to Garsdale, start to stop with about 500 tons, was covered in 30 minutes; not exactly a record but not too bad — or was I influenced by the fact that I was on the footplate?

Jim Carter

No. 6230 DUCHESS OF BUCCLEUCH

Although five streamliners were named after Duchesses, most people feel that it was the appearance of the non-streamlined engines, Nos. 6230–4 which established the 'Duchess' nickname for the class. At first, only the non-streamliners were referred to as 'Duchesses' but eventually, when all members of the class conformed (more or less) to the same outline, the name tended to apply to all of them, although 'Coronation' Class was the official designation. No. 6230 was the first of the non-streamliners to appear and slipped into service quietly with its four identical companions. After a year or so at Camden, it went off to Polmadie and remained there until scrapped. In 1945, the engine was involved in a tender change with No. 6224 and retained an ex-streamlined tender for the rest of its career.

Summary:
Built: Crewe, 27th June, 1938; total cost £10,659
Tenders: 9748 (new); 9707 (1945)
Boilers: first – 10301; last – 10694 (1962); number of boiler changes: 8
Main Shed Allocations: Camden (1938); Polmadie (1940)
Average Annual Mileage: 59,764
Withdrawn: week ending 9th November, 1963

Plate 52: (left, above) No. 6230 at Shrewsbury on running-in duty in 1938 wearing the special 'Duchess' version of the standard LMS livery with gilt and vermilion lining and fitted with single chimney.
Real Photographs

Plate 53: (left, below) By 1948, No. 46230 had acquired smoke deflectors and double chimney and was also one of several painted in experimental BR blue with LNWR style lining. Its tender is by now the ex-streamlined type.
Real Photographs

Plates 54 & 55: (opposite) From 1952, No. 46230 ran in BR standard green and, like all the Scottish-based 'Duchesses', never received the later red livery. In the upper view the engine is seen climbing Beattock with a light-weight train in the early 1950s while below c1957, it is seen at Carlisle with the up 'Royal Scot'.
W. J. V. Anderson & Eric Treacy

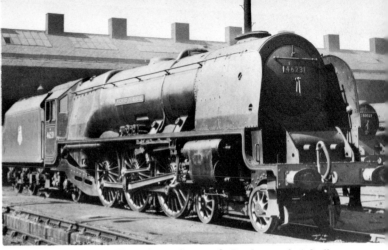

No. 6231 DUCHESS OF ATHOLL

Those of us who were schoolboys during the 1940s will have fond memories of No. 6231, for this was the choice of name and number for that superb Hornby Dublo model which so whetted our appetites in the austerity post-war years. I think the set cost £10 – a small fortune in those days – and I never had one! But I always had a soft spot for '31' as we tended to call it. Like No. 6230, *Duchess of Atholl* went to Polmadie early in its life and stayed there. It too acquired an ex-streamline tender in 1945 and, after being painted BR green in the early 1950s, never changed its livery again. Sadly *Duchess of Atholl* was one of the first three to be scrapped at the end of 1962.

Plates 56 to 58: The three faces of *Duchess of Atholl*. Above left, the engine is as built with single chimney in LMS photographic grey. Left, this 1945 view shows the then new pairing with tender No. 9812 (ex-No. 6249), only partly de-streamlined; the engine now has a double chimney. Smoke deflectors were added later and (right, above) the engine is seen in BR standard livery.

British Rail (LMR) & Real Photographs (2)

Summary:
Built: Crewe, 28th June, 1938; total cost £10,659
Tenders: 9749 (new); 9812 (1945)
Boilers: first — 10302; last — 10646 (1961); number of boiler changes: 8
Main Shed Allocations: Camden (1938); Polmadie (1940)
Average Annual Mileage: 60,100
Withdrawn: week ending 29th December, 1962

Plate 59: In early BR days, No. 46231 was painted experimental BR blue with LNWR lining. It is seen here in this scheme leaving Carlisle for the north in 1949 with rebuilt 'Royal Scot' No. 46105 *Cameron Highlander* alongside.

Gavin Wilson

Plate 60: (above) A fine action shot of *Duchess of Atholl* taking water at speed from Dillicar troughs during the 1950s.

Photomatic

Plate 61: (below) The final appearance with later BR tender emblem is well shown in this broadside view of the engine passing Crawford with a morning Glasgow to Birmingham train. The characteristics of the ex-streamlined tender are shown off very clearly in this view.

David Anderson

Plate 62: *Duchess of Montrose* in original configuration passes Crewe with what, for a 'Duchess' was a rather short train! Obviously the engine is not working particularly hard.

Real Photographs

Plates 63 & 64: These two lovely atmospheric shots were taken at Euston in the late afternoon on a day in 1949 when No. 46232 was wearing experimental BR blue livery and Polmadie shed was still 27A. (It became BR 66A in 1950).

Gavin Wilson

No. 6232 DUCHESS OF MONTROSE

Duchess of Montrose was the third member of the trio of non-streamliners which, after a year or so at Camden, made Polmadie their permanent home. Unlike Nos. 6230/1, however, No. 6232 never changed its tender. Interestingly, all three of them received experimental BR blue while at Polmadie and there are persistent stories that at this former bastion of the Caledonian Railway someone had found a few cans of 'you-know whose' shade of blue paint! One thing seems quite well established. According to contemporary observers the Polmadie blue 'Duchesses' seemed to be a different colour from anyone else's for a while, until officialdom took a hand. We shall never really know now, but it's a nice story! No. 6232 was damaged by enemy action in 1940 and was one of only two members of the class to be withdrawn carrying its original boiler (albeit after having run with many others in the interim period).

Summary:

Built: Crewe, 1st July, 1938; total cost £10,659
Tender: 9750 throughout
Boilers: first — 10303; last — 10303 (1960); number of boiler changes: 8
Main Shed Allocations: Camden (1938); Polmadie (1940)
Average Annual Mileage: 57,998
Withdrawn: week ending 29th December, 1962

Plate 65: *(above)* Framed between a 'Duchess' and a 'Class 5' with at least three more 'Duchesses' in the background, No. 46232 is turned at Crewe North.

Jim Carter

Plate 66: *(below)* *Duchess of Montrose* heads into the hills in the evening sunshine near Elvanfoot with the up 'West Coast Postal' c1960.

David Anderson

No. 6233 DUCHESS OF SUTHERLAND

When Nos. 6230–2 went off to Polmadie in 1940, the two remaining engines remained at Camden and there-after lived a slightly more varied life. No. 6233 went to Crewe in 1944 and spent most of its time there until 1960 when, quite uniquely, it became the only 'Duchess' to be allocated to Edge Hill for anything like a continuous period — at least as far as records show. The engine, like *Duchess of Hamilton* was preserved by Butlins Ltd. and is now based at Bressingham, Norfolk, beautifully restored to pre-war LMS colours.

Summary:
Built: Crewe, 18th July, 1938; total cost £10,659
Tender: 9751 throughout
Boilers: first — 10304; last — 10641 (1959); number of boiler changes: 8
Main Shed Allocations: Camden (1938); Crewe (1944); Edge Hill (1960)
Average Annual Mileage: 67,113
Withdrawn for preservation: week ending 8th February, 1964

Plate 68: In *Power of the Duchesses* I repro-duced part of this picture. Here is the whole view, taken at Upperby, of the up 'Royal Scot' leaving Carlisle with No. 46233.

Eric Treacy

Plate 69: (above) Duchess of Sutherland, in its Edge Hill days, is seen here departing from Chester with a North Wales train.

Jim Carter

Plates 70 & 71: When originally preserved, No. 6233 was painted in LMS crimson and displayed at the Heads of Ayr holiday camp for almost ten years. During that time it appeared as shown right. The forms of insignia given were pretty but quite unlike anything ever carried by an LMS engine. On arrival at Bressingham, historical accuracy prevailed and the view below shows the engine on 21st July, 1974, and as currently displayed.

Jim Carter & John Edgington

No. 6234 DUCHESS OF ABERCORN

Duchess of Abercorn was undoubtedly one of the more celebrated members of the class. During trials in 1939, this engine, when opened out, indicated some 3,300hp at the cylinders — a figure never surpassed by a British express steam locomotive. Subsequently, other members of the class came close (notably No. 46225 in the 1955 tests) but No. 6234 is the one which is remembered as confirming the power potential of the design. These trials resulted also in the fitting of double chimneys to the 'Duchesses'.

After the war, No. 6234 became unique in another way. It was chosen as 'guinea pig' for a proposed new LMS livery — blue/grey with maroon/straw lining. Only one other engine ('Jubilee' No. 5573 *Newfoundland*) was similarly painted but the LMS finally chose glossy black. However, No.

6234 seems to have served its time out, prior to BR days, in the experimental scheme. Some of us felt that No. 6234 should have been selected to be the officially preserved example, but it was not to be.

Summary:
Built: Crewe, 4th August, 1938; total cost £10,659
Tender: 9752 throughout
Boilers: first — 10305; last — 12470 (1959); number of boiler changes: 7
Main Shed Allocations: Camden (1938); Crewe (1943); Camden (1959); Upperby (1959);
Average Annual Mileage: 69,678
Withdrawn: week ending 26th January, 1963

Plates 74 to 76: The blue/grey No. 6234 went into service with, by all accounts, lining applied on the right hand side only. The view (above, left) of the engine at Thrimby Grange c 1947 seems to confirm this, there being no lining apparent on the side illustrated. Above right, at Carlisle, the BR standard green is carried and there is some evidence that the engine went straight from LMS blue/grey to standard green. Below, the engine is seen in its final form in the Scottish foothills on 'Royal Scot' duty.

Eric Treacy (2) & David Anderson

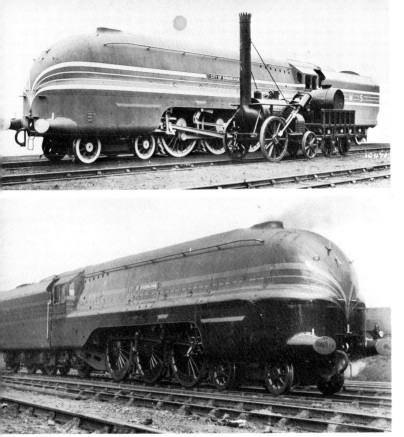

No. 6235 CITY OF BIRMINGHAM

Obviously, the publicity people were not totally convinced by the non-streamliners and in 1939 the LMS reverted to the streamlined form with No. 6235. This engine was built with double chimney from new and also started the 'City' series of engine names. But the enthusiasts continued to call them 'Duchesses' whatever their names or, alternatively, 'Coros'.

City of Birmingham was the first for no other reason than that the city names were planned to be in alphabetical order. No. 6235 was painted red to match the crimson streamlined livery of Nos. 6225–9 and this then became the standard scheme for the streamliners, until wartime forced a change.

City of Birmingham herself was the first streamliner to have the casings removed in 1945 and, smokebox apart, revealed that underneath there was a 'Duchess' waiting to get out! Ultimately, the engine was selected for official preservation, mainly because of its promise of accommodation by its namesake city in a new museum where it remains for all to see.

Plates 77 & 78: No. 6235 in works grey and crimson lake respectively. The reason for posing it alongside the *Rocket* replica is not known. (Incidentally, parts of this replica are incorporated in the new *Rocket* replica built for the National Railway Museum in 1979).

British Rail (LMR) & Author's Collection

Summary:
Built: Crewe, 27th June, 1939; total cost £10,838
Tender: 9798 throughout
Boilers: first – 10287; last – 9940 (1961); number of boiler changes: 8
Main Shed Allocations: Camden (1939); Crewe (1944)
Average Annual Mileage: 63,946
Withdrawn for preservation: week ending 12th September, 1964

Plates 79 & 80: When originally de-streamlined, the LMS had not established its post-war express livery. So No. 6235 came out in unlined black but at least the city crests were applied above the nameplates. A broadside view is shown (left) and the engine is seen leaving Crewe (below) on a West of England working.

Real Photographs

Plate 81: Milk train duties at Golborne in its final years. The engine is in rather scruffy BR green.

Jim Carter

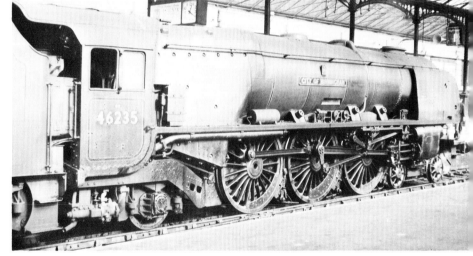

Plate 82: This view of No. 46235, newly arrived at Euston, gives a very clear view of the details at the cab end of a 'Duchess' and should be of help to modellers.

David Anderson

Plate 83: City of Birmingham remained in BR green until scrapping and this view at Crewe station shows the engine just before withdrawal. Electrification wires are well in evidence.

Jim Carter

Plate 84: Dignity and impudence. The almost brand-new *City of Bradford* stands alongside a newly outshopped ex-LNWR 'Coal' tank No. 27586 built at Crewe some 50 years earlier. In a sense this picture truly symbolises the LMS railway — the contrast could hardly be more marked.

Real Photographs

No. 6236 CITY OF BRADFORD

City of Bradford was the engine chosen to represent the class in the BR 1948 locomotive exchanges and in consequence was seen in a wide variety of far-flung places. I have chosen to emphasise this aspect of its activities on these two pages.

On its home metals, No. 6236 spent about half its career at Camden, dividing the rest of its time between Crewe and Upperby from which latter establishment it was withdrawn.

Summary:
  Built: Crewe, 27th July, 1939; total cost £10,838
  Tenders: 9799 (new); 9749 (1949); 9807 (1952)
  Boilers: first — 10288, last — 10301 (1962); number
    of boiler changes: 7
  Main Shed Allocations: Camden (1939); Crewe (1944);
    Camden (1951); Upperby (1958)
  Average Annual Mileage: 66,642
  Withdrawn: week ending 14th March, 1964

Plates 85 & 86: On LNER metals in 1948. The only real rivals to the LMS 'Duchesses' were the Gresley 'A4s' so the performance of No. 46236, newly de-streamlined, must have been of great interest at King's Cross in 1948. The late C. J. Allen (very much an LNER man) summed up the

'Duchess' v 'A4' controversy as 'honours easy'. In the trials, the 'A4s' tested were marginally more economical; the only 'Duchess' involved was much more reliable. I leave the reader to arbitrate. The views here show, above, *City of Bradford* at Finsbury Park on a preliminary trip on 29th April and below, leaving King's Cross with the 1.10pm to Leeds on 6th May.

Photomatic & British Rail (LMR)

Plates 87 & 88: A locomotive designed by an 'escapee' from Swindon must have been equally interesting at Paddington and, above, No. 46236 is seen on 19th May, 1948, approaching the GWR terminus with the 8.30 am from Plymouth, ex-GWR dynamometer car attached. A month later, the same dynamometer car and engine — but with ex-WD tender because of the lack of water troughs on the SR — are seen approaching Vauxhall with the 'Atlantic Coast Express' on the 22nd June trial run.

Gavin Wilson Collection & Photomatic

Plate 89: No. 46236 eventually became a red engine again in 1958, but the view, below shows it in 1957 in BR green on an early down trip of the newly introduced 'Caledonian' express.

British Rail (LMR)

Plates 90 to 92: De-streamlined *City of Bristol* in LMS post-war lined black with BR number (top), BR standard blue (above) and BR green with full cylindrical smokebox at Watford in 1959 (right). This engine was one of the last to lose the short-lived BR blue scheme, and is believed to have carried it until c1955.

Real Photographs (2) & British Rail (LMR)

No. 6237 CITY OF BRISTOL

City of Bristol, like most of the 6235–44 series, came into service during the autumn and winter of 1939–40, so photographic records of its earlier days are much rarer than for those engines built in 1937–8. She was obviously a good performer, having notched up some 1½ million miles by the end of 1959 with an average annual mileage second only to No. 6239. During most of this time, the engine was Camden-based, interrupted by a short spell on the WR in 1955 and then moved to Upperby in mid-1958. It was one of the last survivors, finally being trapped in the autumn 1964 slaughter of the 'Duchesses'.

Summary:
Built: Crewe, 9th August, 1939; total cost £10,838
Tenders: 9800 throughout (except for 9804 during April/May 1944)
Boilers: first – 10289; last – 10645 (1959); number of boiler changes: 7
Main Shed Allocations: Camden (1939); Upperby (1958)
Average Annual Mileage: 72,437
Withdrawn: week ending 12th September, 1964

Plate 93: Another view of No. 46237 at Watford on 9th October, 1959, (see Plate 92). The train was the Euston-Perth and the engine was allocated to Upperby at this time.

British Rail (LMR)

Plate 94: (above) Final days at Crewe North. The yellow cabside stripe was applied to the surviving 'Duchesses' in 1964 as a visual reminder of their prohibition from 'under the wires' south of Crewe.

Jim Carter

Plate 95: (below) A somewhat earlier view at Winwick shows one of the tasks increasingly allocated to 'Duchesses' in their final years — fitted freight. They did it very well.

Jim Carter

No. 6238 CITY OF CARLISLE

City of Carlisle, the first wartime-built 'Duchess', was always one of my favourites — possibly because of its name; the fact that it was red in BR days (and located for much of its time at Upperby), and because it often hauled excursions over the Settle-Carlisle line in its last years. Along with Nos. 6226/8, it was one of the semi-permanent inhabitants of Upperby and always seemed to be kept rather cleaner than most. It survived to the end and, had I been a rich man, I would have liked to have bought this one.

Summary:
Built: Crewe, 14th September, 1939; total cost £10,838
Tender: 9801 throughout
Boilers: first — 10290; last — 10287 (1961); number of boiler changes: 7
Main Allocations: Crewe, then Camden (1939); Upperby (1947)
Average Annual Mileage: 65,951
Withdrawn: week ending 12th September, 1964

Plates 96 to 98: As a streamliner, No. 6238 was a Camden engine and is seen (top) in grubby wartime black with cutback tender side sheets and nameplate removed. By 1947 (above) No. 6238 had transferred to Upperby where it looked quite smart in the 1946 LMS livery. Below in final BR red, the engine poses at Crewe North MPD — still quite clean.

Author's Collection, Real Photographs & Jim Carter

Plate 99: (above) A proper 'Duchess' job — 16 coaches, a 'feather' at the safety valves and a clean engine! No. 46238 at Winwick c1961.

Jim Carter

Plates 100 & 101: (right) City of Carlisle in her final years. Above, the engine is seen at Golborne on freight duty while, below, No. 46238 is leaving Manchester with a Scotland-bound train. The leading pair of coaches is very interesting — one of the articulated pairs from the ill-fated 1939—40 'Coronation Scot' sets destined never to run as complete trains in Britain.

Jim Carter (2)

No. 6239 CITY OF CHESTER

City of Chester, built out of sequence ahead of No. 6238, was yet another member of the class which just quietly got on with its task. It went to Camden when new and, to all intents and purposes, stayed there except for the last year of its life when it re-allocated to Holyhead. It was the only engine of the class to go to 7C for any extended period as far as official records indicate. Its average annual revenue mileage was the best of the class — for the years when records were kept — and its other claim to fame is that its original tender (9802) was exchanged with that from *Duchess of Hamilton* in 1945, so the preserved No. 46229 is now paired with No. 6239's original tender.

Summary:
    Built: Crewe, 29th August, 1939; total cost £10,838
    Tenders: 9802 (new); 9749 (1945)
    Boilers: first — 10291; last — 10306 (1959); number of boiler changes: 7
    Main Shed Allocations: Camden (1939); Willesden from 1961; Holyhead (1963)
    Average Annual Mileage: 76,256
    Withdrawn: week ending 12th September, 1964

Plates 102 to 104: No. 6239 de-streamlined and in post-war LMS colours (left above), was photographed carrying a Willesden shedplate (not recorded on the history card). Left, below, the engine passes Willesden at much the same time. The main picture shows No. 46329 newly equipped with full cylindrical smokebox in March 1957 leaving Carlisle shortly afterwards. Interestingly the engine still carries the older tender emblem, superseded in 1956!

Real Photographs, Gavin Wilson & Eric Treacy

Plate 105: The down 'Royal Scot' at Hest bank in April 1960. At this time it was running in a lightweight formation, which was not to the liking of all its patrons.

British Rail (LMR)

Plate 106: City of Chester at Crewe North **MPD** has either come off the down 'Mid-Day Scot' – or is about to take over the up working of this train.

Jim Carter

Plate 107: Southbound over Bushey troughs on 6th April, 1963, No. 46239 is in charge of an England v Scotland football special.

Gerald Robinson

Plate 108: *City of Coventry* hauling a 17 coach wartime train near Golborne. The tender has not yet had the side sheets cut back which means that, unbelievably, this scruffy creature is still red!

Coopers Railway Photographs

No. 6240 CITY OF COVENTRY

Like *City of Chester*, No. 6240 was another highly consistent Camden performer. From early 1940 to scrapping in 1964, the engine was never located away from London. It was never, as far as is known, given any experimental liveries but was one of the last to retain the BR blue livery (until at least 1954). Also, it probably only ran in BR green for one period between works visits before it was painted red in 1958. It was one of the last three 'Duchesses' to remain in the London area. (The others were *City of Lancaster* and *City of London*). I recall seeing all of them for the last time during 1963 by which time they had taken up residence at Willesden after Camden was closed in 1961.

Summary:
Built: Crewe, 27th March, 1940; total cost £10,838
Tenders: 9803 (new); 9703 (1944); 9803 (1944)
Boilers: first – 10292; last – 9941 (1962); number of boiler changes: 7
Main Shed Allocations: Camden throughout (Willesden after 1961).
Average Annual Mileage: 70,949
Withdrawn: week ending 12th September, 1964

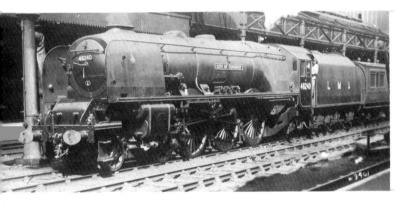

Plates 109 & 110: Like many of the class, No. 6240 received its new BR number whilst still wearing LMS livery (above). It was also one of the last to be fitted with a fully cylindrical smokebox (1957). It was seen at about this time at Carlisle (below) at the head of a Perth-Euston train.

Real Photographs & Eric Treacy

Plate 111: Crewe works was a bit late in adopting the new BR tender emblem (introduced in 1956) and many 'Duchesses' (including No. 46240) probably retained the old style device until repainting in BR red livery. This view of the down 'Mid-Day Scot' was taken at Preston in June 1957.

Photomatic

Plate 112: Twilight of steam on Camden bank. *City of Coventry* is seen with the 5.37pm Euston-Heysham relief on 24th July, 1964, shortly before the class was banned south of Crewe.

Gerald Robinson

Plate 113: Unless the lining is of the LMS style, it is difficult to recognise the BR red livery on a black and white picture but this picture of No. 46240 at Elvanfoot almost certainly shows the engine in BR red with BR type lining, as the later tender emblem seems to indicate.

David Anderson

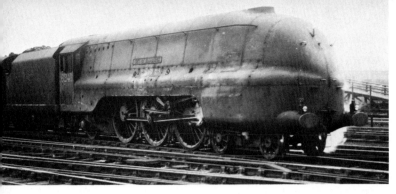

Plates 115 & 116: These two views show No. 46241 de-streamlined with the depressed smokebox top. In the upper view the engine is seen leaving Kensal Green tunnel in 1948, painted experimental BR blue with LNWR lining, while below it is brought to a signal stop at Bletchley in 1957 with a lightweight up express.

R. W. Beaton & D. Jenkinson

No. 6241 CITY OF EDINBURGH

City of Edinburgh was yet another of the 6235–44 series to notch up some remarkable mileage figures in traffic, coming third in order after Nos. 6239 and 6237. This series of engines was proved to be very good in mileage terms, although their location at Camden for much of their lives may be the significant factor, since the London-based duties were often very demanding in terms of daily mileage.

Summary:
    Built: Crewe, 3rd April, 1940; total cost £10,838
    Tenders: 9804 (new); 9805 (1944); 9811 (1953);
        9703 (1956); 9811 (1956)
    Boilers: first — 10293; last — 10643 (1958); number
        of boiler changes: 6
    Main Shed Allocations: Crewe, then Camden (1940);
        Crewe (1958)
    Average Annual Mileage: 72, 202
    Withdrawn: week ending 5th September, 1964

Plate 117: (opposite, top) ▷ In charge of the up 'Caledonian' on Beattock summit in 1958 is *City of Edinburgh*. Soon afterwards, the engine was transferred to Crewe North.

Eric Treacy

Plate 118: (opposite, ▷ *below)* For a very short time in 1957, No. 46241 was officially allocated to Edge Hill for boat train duties. This view was taken much later — note the fully cylindrical smokebox and electrification flashes — but the engine has an 8A shedplate again — a move not recorded on its history card.

Jim Carter

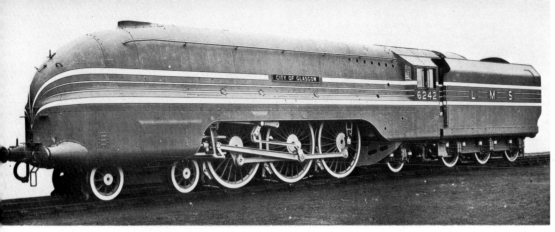

Plate 122: (opposite) Seen here, ▷ heading south from Tebay in 1962 is *City of Glasgow*. Note the cloud of steam at the back of the tender denoting that the coal pusher was in use at the time.

Gavin Wilson

Plates 119 & 120: (left) No. 6242 in LMS days before and after de-streamlining. The upper view shows the locomotive in works grey and the cowling above the front part of the tender coal space is clearly visible. This characteristic feature of all the red streamliners, which was retrospectively applied to the blue ones, was possibly to stop dust swirling into the cab. The lower view shows the engine in post-war LMS lined black livery.

*British Rail (LMR) &
Author's Collection*

No. 6242 CITY OF GLASGOW

This engine had the unique distinction of being the only member of the class to sport both the utility-type front footplate of the de-streamlined form and the full footplate style of the 6230–4/6249–52 series. This occurred because it was almost totally rebuilt after the 1952 Harrow disaster — the only engine of the three involved to survive. It was also one of very few members of the class to spend reasonably continuous periods at all the principal 'Duchess' depots and was finally withdrawn from Polmadie. It also underwent a bewildering number of tender changes but not many changes of livery. It retained BR green to the last.

Summary:
Built: Crewe, 15th May, 1940: total cost £10,838
Tenders: 9805 (new); 9804 (1944); 9800 (1944);
9804 (1944); 9703 (1946); 9816 (1951); 9703 (1951);
9811 (1956); 9703 (1956)
Boilers: first — 10294 ; last — 10639 (1959); number of
boiler changes: 6
Main Shed Allocations: Camden (1940); Polmadie (1944);
Camden (1948); Crewe (1953); Camden (1954);
Polmadie (1961)
Average Annual Mileage: 68,818
Withdrawn: week ending 19th October, 1963

Plate 121: (left) This picture shows No. 46242 with the full front footplate arrangement at Golborne on the inaugural run of the down 'Caledonian' — the nearest BR ever came to emulating the pre-war 'Coronation Scot'.

Photomatic

Plate 123: (opposite) This view ▷ shows *City of Glasgow* during its final Polmadie-based days hauling empty stock at Perth on 17th June, 1962.

Gerald Robinson

No. 6243 CITY OF LANCASTER

City of Lancaster was probably most celebrated because it was the last to be de-streamlined (in 1949), thus going direct from drab black to BR standard blue. Thereafter, however, it was given all the BR 'Duchess' liveries in turn, including both versions of BR red. Its working life was divided mostly between London and Crewe and it was one of the last three of this type to be based in the London area.

Summary:
Built: Crewe, 29th May, 1940; total cost £10,838
Tender: 9806 throughout
Boilers: first — 10295; last — 10290 (1961); number of boiler changes: 8
Main Shed Allocations: Camden (1940); Edge Hill (1948); Crewe (1948); Upperby (1958); Crewe (1958); Camden, later Willesden (1960)
Average Annual Mileage: 64,810
Withdrawn: week ending 12th September, 1964

Plates 127 to 129: Later views of *City of Lancaster*. At the top it is seen in BR green in the mid-1950s. Note that the cab front windows have been enlarged. The middle picture shows it in BR maroon at Carnforth in July 1964 carrying an Edge Hill shed-plate — an allocation not recorded on its official record cards. Finally, it is seen in the Crawford area on a south-bound express and the writer would dearly like to be able to identify the fourth coach in the train — suggestions, please, via the publisher!

Author's Collection
Photomatic &
David Anderson

Plates 130 to 132: King George VI in early days. Top, left, the engine is seen in unlined black, still streamlined c1944–5, while above, it displays the full post-war LMS style after de-streamlining in late 1947. The view on Whitmore troughs (left) shows the engine in BR blue, probably late 1948/early 1949, since most of the carriages are still in LMS colours. This engine was the prototype for the standard BR blue scheme and was originally lined black/yellow rather than black/white.

Real Photographs (3)

Plate 133: (below) After BR green, No. 46244 was painted red and this view, taken in 1959, shows the engine in red livery at Euston. At this time the lining was in BR style (not LMS). This can be discerned from the original picture.

British Rail (LMR)

No. 6244 KING GEORGE V1

No. 6244 came into service as the last of the red streamliners and was originally named *City of Leeds*. However, early in 1941, it was renamed for patriotic reasons. The engine was always one of the star Camden performers and frequently, for obvious reasons, found itself on Royal Train duty. It went to Upperby in mid-1958 and remained there until all the surviving engines were withdrawn from Carlisle in late 1964. This engine was responsible for probably the fastest ever post-war long distance 'Duchess' performance on a scheduled train when it brought the up 'Caledonian' the 299 miles from Carlisle to Euston in a net time of 242 minutes on 5th September, 1957, gaining 37 minutes on the schedule and averaging 74 mph. Sadly, no detailed record was taken — only the guard's log — so precise details of speeds cannot be ascertained but in some respects this performance was better than the record run in 1937 by No. 6220.

Summary:

Built: Crewe, 12th July, 1940; total cost £10,838
Tenders: 9807 (new); 9808 (1945)
Boilers: first — 10296; last — 10644 (1960); number of boiler changes: 7
Main Shed Allocations: Camden (1940); Upperby (1958)
Average Annual Mileage: 71,495
Withdrawn: week ending 12th September, 1964

Plate 134: No. 46244 climbing southbound up to Shap in the days when Upperby was coded 12A. The engine would have been painted red at this time.

Eric Treacy

Plate 135: At the Crewe works centenary on 2nd September, 1943, the official group photograph was taken in front of the then fairly new *City of London.*

British Rail (LMR)

Plates 136 & 137: City of London on the troughs. At the left the engine heads the down 'Royal Scot' at Bushey on what is believed to be the centenary run of the 10.00 from Euston on 16th February, 1948. Below, a few months later, another Glasgow train is seen on Whitmore troughs with the engine now carrying BR number but still in post-war LMS colours.

*British Rail (LMR) &
Real Photographs*

No. 6245 CITY OF LONDON

In theory, when 'Duchess' building resumed in 1943, No. 6245 could have taken the displaced *City of Leeds* name (see No. 6244, previous page). However, the LMS got itself into a terrible muddle with its naming programme with the last series of 'Cities' and the ordered sequence was broken. *City of London* was the first of the black streamliners but in 1957 honour was satisfied when the engine became the first to be painted BR maroon — always with LMS-style lining, never the BR pattern. With *City of Coventry* and *City of Lancaster*. No. 46245 was one of the last three 'Duchesses' to be based in London. Interestingly, it underwent only four boiler changes during its working life.

Summary:
    Built: Crewe, 26th June, 1943; total cost £10,919
    Tenders: 9808 (new); 9807 (1945); 9811 (1952); 9805 (1953)
    Boilers: first — 9940 (2nd hand); last — 10292 (1956); number of boiler changes: 4
    Main Shed Allocations: Camden throughout (Willesden from 1961)
    Average Annual Mileage: 68,968
    Withdrawn: week ending 12th September, 1964

Plates 138 & 139: Both these pictures were taken at Crewe North in 1948 and 1964, respectively. Above, the locomotive is in experimental colours (blue or black) and, below, is carrying the yellow stripe prohibition mark banning its use over electrified routes. In both cases a 5A shedplate is carried yet, according to the record cards, No. 46245 was never allocated to Crewe!

Author's Collection & Jim Carter

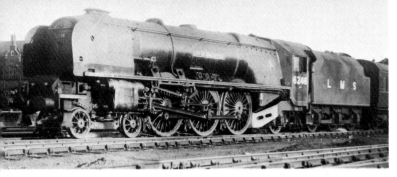

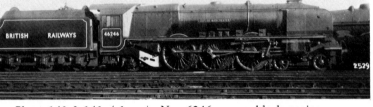

No. 6246 CITY OF MANCHESTER

City of Manchester was interesting in several respects. It was one of the eight members of the class to average over 70,000 revenue miles per year (for the years when records were kept) yet, in spite of this, was one of the first to be withdrawn, early in 1963. This somewhat unwelcome distinction was shared with *City of Liverpool*. No. 46246 was also the last member to lose its sloping smokebox top (1960); and the only one to be repainted maroon (with BR-style lining) with this feature for the 7 months from October 1959 to May 1960.

Summary:
Built: Crewe, 11th August, 1943; total cost £11,777
Tenders: 9809 (new); 9749 (1961)
Boilers: first — 10645; last — 9937 (1960); number of boiler changes: 6
Main Shed Allocations: Camden (1943); Crewe (1948); Camden, later Willesden (1960)
Average Annual Mileage: 71,256
Withdrawn: week ending 26th January, 1963

Plates 140 & 141: (above) No. 6246 was a black engine for more than half its lifetime. Above, the two black de-streamlined liveries are shown, LMS post-war and BR experimental, lined LNWR fashion.

Real Photographs

Plates 142 & 143: (below) The engine was not painted green until 1954 and was never blue. It is seen at Polmadie (below) in BR green c1956. Finally, in May 1960, it achieved a fully cylindrical smokebox and BR red livery, lined LMS style. This is seen in the bottom picture at Symington on the up 'Mid-Day Scot' shortly before an exchange of tenders with No. 46247.

David Anderson

No. 6247 CITY OF LIVERPOOL

In spite of its name, No. 6247 was a London-based engine all its working life and was one of three 'Duchesses' – 6245/8 were the others – which entered service when new with second-hand boilers. Nevertheless, the engine was always a good performer. It was one of several ex-streamliners to be paired, in turn, with the non-streamlined tender originally fitted to No. 6231 and carried it for the longest period (1952–61). Like *City of Manchester* No. 46247 was withdrawn early in spite of its high annual mileage figures.

Summary:

Built: Crewe, 13th September, 1943; total cost £10,632

Tenders: 9810 (new); 9811 (1944); 9807 (1952); 9749 (1952); 9809 (1961)

Boilers: first – 10303 (2nd hand); last – 12472 (1959); number of boiler changes: 5

Main Shed Allocations: Camden throughout (Willesden from 1961)

Average Annual Mileage: 70,574

Withdrawn: week ending 25th May, 1963

Plates 144 & 145: (above)   City of Liverpool near the start and finish of its career as a wartime black streamliner (upper); and as a red ex-streamliner at Hest bank in August 1961 (lower).   *Real Photographs & Author's Collection*

Plates 146 & 147: (below)   City of Liverpool was never, as far as the author is aware, painted in either BR experimental colours or BR standard blue. During its early BR years it appeared as in the upper view (i.e. LMS post-war colours) and retained them until 1953, latterly with BR crest on the tender. The bottom picture shows it at Crawford in maroon with BR lining, paired with the non-streamline tender it later exchanged with No. 46246.   *A. Noble & David Anderson*

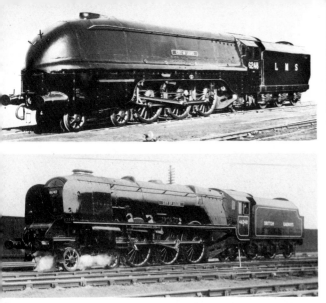

Plates 148 to 150: Three views of *City of Leeds* in early days. Top left sees it as built before the tender side-sheets were cut back. Above it is in LMS post-war colours at Glasgow very early in 1948. Later that year (left) it received the experimental BR lined black scheme.

British Rail (LMR), Gavin Wilson & Real Photographs

No. 6248 CITY OF LEEDS

The *City of Leeds* nameplates (see No. 6244) re-appeared on No. 6248, the last of the streamliners which, like Nos. 6245/7, was built with a re-conditioned boiler. It exchanged streamlined tenders with No. 6247 very early in life and thereafter ran the gamut of all the subsequent LMS/BR changes in configuration and livery. It notched up some creditable annual mileage figures coming 9th in the class — a high ranking for an engine which spent relatively little of its life at Camden. While at Crewe it spent occasional period on short detachments to Upperby and Camden.

Summary:
Built: Crewe, 2nd October, 1943; total cost £11,040
Tenders: 9811 (new); 9810 (1944)
Boilers: first — 10638 (2nd hand); last — 10294 (1959); number of boiler changes: 6
Main Shed Allocations: Camden (1943); Crewe (1948)
Average Annual Mileage: 69,944
Withdrawn: week ending 5th September, 1964

Plate 151: *City of Leeds* in BR green livery taking water north-bound at Dillicar in the early 1950s.

Photomatic

Plates 152 & 153: *City of Leeds* was a Crewe-based engine for most of its life and in its later years was nearly always beautifully turned out. With No. 46234, it seems to have been the 'flower' of the Crewe allocation. Above, it is seen heading north at Watford and, below, it is waiting its turn of duty at Chester. Both pictures are c1960/61 and show the engine in BR maroon livery.

British Rail (LMR) & Jim Carter

Plates 154 & 155: (above) For a short time in 1945, No. 6249 ran with the original tender of No. 6231 (left), but by the time the engine acquired smoke deflectors and 1946 livery (right) it had received the ex-streamlined tender from No. 6225.

British Rail (LMR) & Real Photographs

No. 6249 CITY OF SHEFFIELD

City of Sheffield was the first of four wartime 'Duchesses' ordered as streamliners but actually built non-streamlined. They were fitted with streamlined tenders (already built) but No. 6249 quickly lost hers to No. 6231. These four engines (Nos. 6249–52) were also the only four of the class not to go immediately to Camden. After a short time at Crewe, No. 6249 went to Scotland and joined the Polmadie group with Nos. 6250/1. *City of Sheffield* spent long periods at all four 'Duchess' depots and returned to Polmadie for the final years.

Summary:
 Built: Crewe, 19th April, 1944; total cost £11,664
 Tenders: 9812 (new); 9749 (1945); 9743 (1945)
 Boilers: first — 10644; last — 10293 (1960); number
  of boiler changes: 6
 Main Shed Allocations: Crewe, then Polmadie (1944);
  Upperby (1946); Camden (1949); Crewe (1954);
  Polmadie (1961)
 Average Annual Mileage: 58,724
 Withdrawn: week ending 9th November, 1963

Plate 156: (left) A rousing start from Carlisle in later years with a West of England train.

Gavin Wilson Collection

Plate 157: (below) With the building of No. 6249, the full footplate front (as on Nos. 6230–4) re-appeared and this is well shown on the view at Acton Bridge heading a Glasgow-Birmingham train in June, 1952.

British Rail (LMR)

No. 6250 CITY OF LICHFIELD

Like Nos. 6249/51, *City of Lichfield* started its main career away from London, going to Polmadie after a short time at Crewe. Of all the class, this engine probably spent less time allocated to the London area than any other, going only occasionally to Camden (for short periods) in the early 1950s and then to Willesden at the very close of its career for a few months. It was one of the earlier examples to be withdrawn.

Summary:
    Built: Crewe, 20th May, 1944; total cost £11,664
    Tenders: 9813 throughout
Boilers: first — 10646; last — 10300 (1961); number of
        boiler changes: 5
    Main Shed Allocations: Crewe, then Polmadie (1944);
    Upperby (1946); Camden (1949); Upperby (1958)
        Average Annual Mileage: 69,057
        Withdrawn: 12th September, 1964

Plate 158: (top) No. 46250 poses at Upperby during its final years. The smoke deflector modification at the lower front edge for this type of footplate front is particularly clearly illustrated.

Author's Collection

Plates 159 & 160: (right & below) Two views in the north. To the right No. 46250 heads south through the hills with the up 'Royal Scot' in the early 1950s while below, in her twilight years, local passenger duty at Warrington is the best which can be offered.

Eric Treacy & Jim Carter

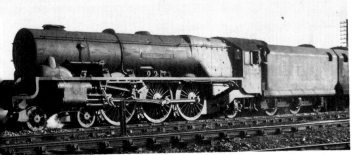

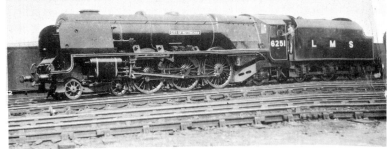

No. 6251 CITY OF NOTTINGHAM

If engines had horoscopes then *City of Nottingham* was a true Gemini, being, for some unaccountable reason, by far the most restless of all the 'Duchesses' in terms of shed re-allocation during the 1940s and 1950s. This was normally the fate of a 'rogue' engine in steam days but the records give no real indication that No. 6251 came into this category. Her mileage figure was a little below average but not excessively so. In her later years she settled down (mainly at Crewe) and became a distinguished and well-known performer — much in demand for rail tours in her last years.

Plate 165: (below) Its wanderings took No. 46251 to Edge Hill, especially in the mid-1950s. It is seen at this time in charge of the up 'Shamrock' at Bletchley.

Lance Brown

Plates 161 to 164: (above) *City of Nottingham* remained black for as long as any other member of the class. Four stages are shown here. Upper left, as built with streamline tender; upper right, LMS post-war; lower left, LMS livery with BR number and, lower right, BR experimental black.

Real Photographs

Summary:
    Built: Crewe, 30th June 1944; total cost £11,664
    Tender: 9814 throughout
Boilers: first — 10693; last — 10295 (1960); number of boiler changes: 5
Main Shed Allocations: Crewe, then Polmadie (1944)
Upperby (1946); Camden, Edge Hill, Crewe (1948);
Camden, Upperby (1949); Camden, Upperby (1950).
often detached to Camden, Edge Hill (1954–6);
Crewe (1956); Upperby, Crewe (1957)
    Average Annual Mileage: 63,250
    Withdrawn: 12th September, 1964

Plates 166 & 167:   Like many Crewe 'Duchesses' in their final years, No. 46251 was always kept in beautiful condition as these pictures testify. Above, the engine, now in BR maroon, poses for a formal portrait; while below, it is seen near Didcot with the RCTS 'East Midlander' rail tour. The now familiar 'heads out of windows' aspect of steam travel was, at that time, a new phenomenon!

Jim Carter & David Anderson

Plates 168 to 170: *City of Leicester* in unlined wartime black in LMS days seen (left top), as built and (left) as first modified with smoke deflectors and partly de-streamlined tender. Above, the engine, in final LMS configuration, approaches Crewe.

British Rail (LMR) & Real Photographs (2)

No. 6252 CITY OF LEICESTER

The last of the four wartime non-streamliners was No. 6252, but it did not share the movements of Nos. 6249–51. It spent its first six years and most of the rest of its time at Crewe. Of all the class, this engine probably spent less time allocated to the London area than any other, going only occasionally to Camden (for short periods) in the early 1950s and then to Willesden at the very close of its career for a few months. It was one of the earlier examples to be withdrawn.

Summary:

Built: Crewe, 24th June, 1944; total cost £11,664
Tender: 9815 throughout
Boilers: first – 10694; last – 10304 (1960); number of boiler changes: 6
Main Shed Allocations: Crewe (1944); Camden, Crewe alternating (1950–2); Upperby, Crewe (1953); Upperby, Crewe (1956); Upperby (1960); Willesden (1962)
Average Annual Mileage: 65,065
Withdrawn: week ending 1st June, 1963

Plate 171: *(below)* Sunlight and shadows at Preston in the early 1960s. The engine is in BR green.
Gavin Wilson Collection

Plates 172 & 173: ▷ *(opposite)* One of eight or nine 'Duchesses' painted in LNWR black during 1948 was *City of Leicester*. The Crewe paintshop was obviously enjoying itself! In the upper view No. 46252 in this colour scheme heads the down 'Mid-Day Scot' at Whitmore. The first three coaches are BR red/cream; BR experimental 'plum/spilt milk', and LMS crimson, respectively. Below, the engine is on the old Caledonian main line at Law Junction in the mid-1950s with a train of mostly BR stock during another coaching stock livery transition – this time from red/cream to maroon.

Real Photographs & Eric Treacy

No. 6253 CITY OF ST. ALBANS

Two 'Duchesses' were cancelled from the 1939 order for twenty engines which would have been numbered 6235–54. So, after the war, the first new order for five engines began with No. 6253 *City of St. Albans*. This was the first non-streamliner to have the 'utility' front footplate combined with cylindrical smokebox. In time, this became the most common form but No. 6253 looked rather different from the rest when first built. This engine also introduced the rivetted tender to the 'Duchess' class. Although in the 'top ten' in annual mileage terms, No. 46253 was an early withdrawal in January 1963.

Summary:
Built: Crewe, 14th September, 1946; total cost £15,460
Tenders: 9816 (new); 9703 (1951); 9816 (1951);
9750 (1954); 9816 (1955); 9704 (1961)
Boilers: first – 12470; last – 13043 (1960); number of
boiler changes: 5
Main Shed Allocations: Camden (1946); Upperby (1949);
Camden (1952); Crewe (1957)
Average Annual Mileage: 70, 107
Withdrawn: week ending 26th January, 1963

Plates 174 & 175: (above) As far as is known, No. 6253 only ever enjoyed two colour schemes, LMS post-war black and BR green – something of a dull existence for a 'Duchess'! The upper view shows the 1946 livery in works grey form (without boiler band lining) while the lower shows BR green in 1959.

British Rail (LMR) & Photomatic

Plate 176: (below) During early BR days, the engine ran in LMS colours with its BR number and is seen here at Preston in August 1949 with a Glasgow to Euston train.

Photomatic

Plate 177: (right) A classic shot of No. 46253 on Beattock with the down 'Royal Scot' in the early 1950s.

Eric Treacy

Plate 178: (below) In the final years No. 46253 was at Crewe North and visited North Wales frequently. During this time it was photographed leaving Chester heading towards the tunnels with a Holyhead train.

Jim Carter

Plate 179: (above) *City of Stoke-on-Trent* on the 1.0pm Euston to Glasgow train south of Apsley on 13th September, 1949, still in LMS colours but with new number.

British Rail (LMR)

Plate 180: (left) It took some time after the war before the standards of cleanliness returned to normal and No. 6254 is distinctly dirty in this late LMS view of the down 'Royal Scot' ascending Shap.

British Rail (LMR)

No. 6254 CITY OF STOKE-ON-TRENT

This engine entered service simultaneously with No. 6253 at Camden and thereafter their careers were rather similar. They both went to Upperby in 1949, back to Camden in the 1950s and served out their times at Crewe. No. 6254 was, however, the more colourful (literally) of the two being given all the various BR liveries in succession from 1951 to 1958. In 1956, No. 46254 was one of the two 'Duchesses' loaned to the Western Region — the other being No. 46257.

Summary:
Built: Crewe, 17th September, 1946; total cost £15,460
Tender: 9817 throughout
Boilers: first — 12471; last — 10642 (1961); number of boiler changes: 5
Main Shed Allocations: Camden (1946); Upperby (1949); Crewe (1952); Upperby, Camden (1953); Crewe (1957)
Average Annual Mileage: 63,760
Withdrawn: week ending 12th September, 1964

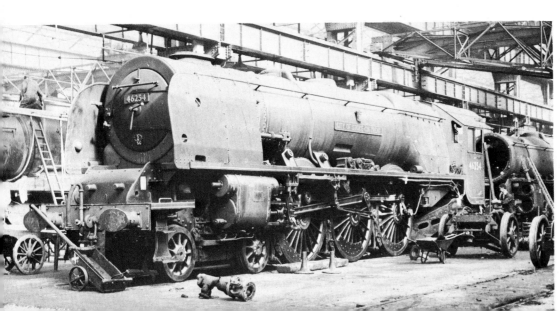

Plate 181: (left) No. 46254 in Crewe workshops almost certainly undergoing its last general overhaul in 1961.

Jim Carter

Plate 182: (opposite) Making ▷ a rousing southbound start from Carlisle, No. 46254 was photographed just prior to its transfer from Camden to Crewe.

Eric Treacy

Plate 183: No. 6255 in the works grey version of the full 1946 LMS livery with lined boiler bands.

British Rail (LMR)

No. 6255 CITY OF HEREFORD

No. 6255 was the last of the three engines built in 1946 and the last of the 'normal' 'Duchesses'. She was essentially a Carlisle engine for most of her life (after a year or two at Camden at the close of the LMS period) and was one of the large batch withdrawn in the autumn of 1964. She was the last 'Duchess' I personally saw working a regular train in BR service during the summer of that year.

Summary:
    Built: Crewe, 16th October, 1946; total cost £15,460
                Tender: 10622 throughout
    Boilers: first — 12472; last — 10305 (1957); number of
                boiler changes: 4
    Main Shed Allocations: Camden (1946); Upperby (1948);
                Crewe (1952); Upperby (1953)
            Average Annual Mileage: 63,398
        Withdrawn: week ending 12th September, 1964

Plate 184: (left) In July 1964, I spent a frustrating day at Dent Head waiting to photograph what I thought at the time would be the last red steam engine I would ever see going over the Settle to Carlisle line — *City of Carlisle* on an 'SLS' special. My camera fired too soon and the engine turned out to be a green No. 46255! In this view the same train is seen approaching Ais Gill a few minutes earlier.

Photomatic

Plate 185: (below) *City of Hereford* on a down express at Wigan.

Jim Carter

No. 6256 SIR WILLIAM A. STANIER, F.R.S.

It was a splendid inspiration on the part of Stanier's colleagues to suggest to the LMS that the last 'Pacific' to be built by the company (and the 50th LMS 4-6-2 counting the 'Princesses' and 'Turbomotive') should be named after the man (now retired from the company) who had designed it. No. 6256 was the first of two 'improved' 'Duchesses' designated as comparators for the new LMS diesels. They embodied several changes to the original design but were still self-evidently Stanier 'Duchesses'. In the event their performance was not markedly different from their predecessors but No. 6256 was the very last to be withdrawn from service and the writer proposes to claim author's privilege in giving the same preferential treatment in this book as has already been accorded to *Duchess of Hamilton* — and for rather similar reasons!

Summary:
Built: Crewe, 13th December, 1947; total cost £21,411
Tender: 10623 throughout
Boilers: first — 12473; last — 13044 (1959); number of boiler changes: 4
Main Shed Allocations: Crewe, then Camden (early 1948); Upperby (1959); Camden (1960); Crewe (1960)
Average Annual Mileage: 63,504
Withdrawn: week ending 3rd October, 1964

Plates 186 & 187: (above) No. 6256 as built in LMS post-war colours. The most obvious visible changes were the new design of trailing truck and the attenuated cab side-sheets.
British Rail (LMR)

Plates 188 & 189: (below) The first post-nationalisation livery was, essentially, LMS post-war black with BR markings (upper), followed late in 1948 by LNWR black (lower). By this time electric headlamps had been fitted, the conduit below the handrail being clearly visible.
Real Photographs (2)

Plates 190 & 191: BR blue (upper) and BR green (lower) were applied in 1952 and, probably, 1954 respectively. Once again, note the connections to the electric headlamps.
Real Photographs (2)

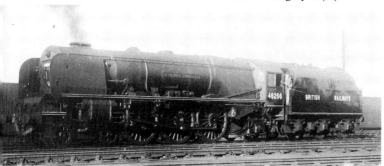

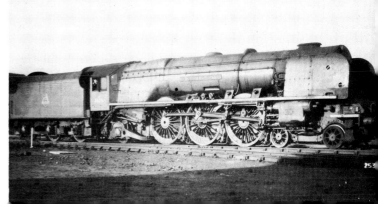

Plate 195: (opposite, top) Another ▷ departure from Carlisle, c 1954–5. Note the electric headlamps replacing the normal oil-lit variety.

Eric Treacy

Plates 192 & 193: (left, top and centre) Leaving Carlisle, 1948. There was another visible detail difference on the utility footplate front on No. 46256. It lacked the vertical valance plate below the steam pipe casings cf Plate 177. This is particularly noticeable in the upper view.

Gavin Wilson & Real Photographs

Plate 196: (opposite, below) This ▷ famous picture has been published several times but it is always worth another showing. The engine is climbing Beattock bank early one summer morning in 1958 with a sleeping car train and is now BR maroon, lined LMS-style. The electric headlamps are there but so are two oil lamps in the express headcode position above the buffers.

W. J. V. Anderson

Plate 194: (left, below) No. 46256 taking a run at Shap from Tebay with the down 'Royal Scot' on 6th May, 1953. The locomotive is still blue.

British Rail (LMR)

Plate 197: (above) This fine panned shot of No. 46256 passing Winwick at speed clearly shows off the slight visual differences between this engine and the early type – cf Plate 113.

Jim Carter

Plate 198: (below) Nearing the end in August 1964, No. 46256 now carries the cab-side prohibition stripe at Thrimby Grange with a Sundays only stopping train to Manchester. Note that the electric lights have been removed and the engine is virtually 'as-built'. A pity she was not preserved.

S. C. Crook

No. 46257 CITY OF SALFORD

City of Salford was the only BR-built 'Duchess' and an identical twin to No. 6256, although somewhat overshadowed by the former engine in popular esteem. Although the shortest-lived of any member, having a working life of only 16 years, the engine was a good performer, putting up annual mileage figures rather better than those of No. 6256. In those 16 years there were only three boilers changes. This engine, like No. 46254, was borrowed by the Western Region in 1956. This was the only engine (apart from No. 46232) to be carrying the original boiler at the time of withdrawal.

Summary:
    Built: Crewe, 19th May, 1948; total cost £21,411
    Tender: 10624 throughout
    Boilers: first — 12474; last — 12474 (1959); number
      of boiler changes: 3
    Main Shed Allocations: Camden (1948); Upperby (1959)
    Average Annual Mileage: 69,548
    Withdrawn: week ending 12th September, 1964

Plates 200 & 201: Like No. 46256, *City of Salford* also carried electric headlamps for a time as seen (right) leaving Kensal Green tunnel in June 1953. In its final years it too had them removed as shown in the picture below at Winwick with a fitted freight train. No. 46257 retained BR green until scrapping.

British Rail (LMR) & Jim Carter

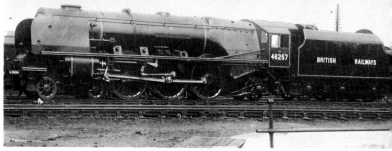

Plate 199: No. 46257 as built. Although given, naturally, the BR markings, it did at least receive LMS livery when new. Note the absence of nameplate at first.

Real Photographs

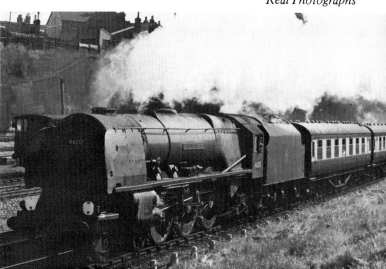

Tailpiece:
Plates 202 & 203: To me, the 'Duchesses' were never more impressive than when hill-climbing in the hands of a sympathetic driver. They did not always get one, of course, but when the man in the left hand seat pushed the lever up to the roof and his fireman also knew what he was doing, then the experience was exhilarating. Happily we can now once again say *is* exhilarating since No. 46229 came back to work. I can, therefore, think of no better way of closing this book than by showing the best of the past: No. 46240 *City of Coventry* climbing Shap in the 1950s (left); and — one of the most impressive sights in the present-day preservation scene — No. 46229 *Duchess of Hamilton* climbing the northern hills once more — (below).

Eric Treacy & David Eatwell